Design and Architecture of SNMP Monitoring System

By

Muhammad Nauman Khan

Tauseef Jamal

Design and Architecture of SNMP Monitoring System

By

Muhammad Nauman Khan

Tauseef Jamal

In the Name of ALLAH, Most Gracious,
Most Merciful

Table of Contents

List of Figures

List of Tables

List of Algorithms

Nomenclature

SNMP	Simple Network Management Protocol
TCP	Transmission Control Protocol
IP	Internet Protocol
ICMP	Internet Control Message Protocol
MIB	Management Information Base
SMI	Structure Management Information
PDU	Protocol Data Unit
CSMS	Cyber Security Monitoring System
RFC	Request for Comments
CIA	Confidentiality, Integrity, Availability
OSI	Open Systems Interconnection
NMS	Network Monitoring System
ISO	International Organization for Standardization
I.T	Information Technology
SIP	Session Initiation Protocol
NTP	Network Time Protocol

Abstract

Today, the number of networks grows within organization and series of devices such as routers, switches, hubs, hosts, servers and bridges etc. from different vendors are added to networks over the time. Due to the growth of networks, monitoring and maintenance for coherent network is an important task for network administrators. A network monitoring is considered to be an essential aspect of any network of any size. The importance of cyber security monitoring rises due to large number of cyber-attacks over the networks. The cyber security monitoring system (CSMS) requires efficient methods to detect threats, risks, failures, faults, inappropriate accesses, and alerts over the networks.

SNMP based monitoring of networks is the efficient method because of the trifling overheads of SNMP operations over the networks. Our project is about designing and development of cyber security monitoring system using SNMP. This monitoring system has an ability to detect threats, faults and alarms related the cyber security space.

The proposed objectives of projects are achieved by incremental development approach. Our project has greater significance in the field of network monitoring and cyber security. It provides the overall design and architecture of SNMP based monitoring system. Our work acts as a base for the development of CSMS and can be extended to enhance its capabilities.

Chapter 1 : Introduction

This chapter gives the introduction to the cyber security monitoring system by discussing the overview of the network monitoring in detail. It also includes the brief, purpose and scope of the project.

1.1 Overview

Over some past years, Networks grew with the addition of series of diverse from different vendors to networks such routers, switches, hubs, and servers etc. As the size and complexity of networks are increased, the importance of network management and monitoring are also raised as a counter factor. Different protocols and standards were developed to accomplish the task of management and monitoring. Large number of attacks to the networks also increased the importance of network monitoring. The organizations took different preventative measures to protect the network assets from potential attacks.

Today, network monitoring is essential aspect in order to monitor the internal networks for problems or threats and preemptively identifies faults related to the network. Earlier detections will be helpful in the reduction of impact of these faults over network. Network monitoring is critical IT function that constantly monitors the network and notifies the administrator about the faults.

Networks face different cyber-attacks that pose devastating threats to networks services and resources. Numbers of tools are freely available used by most of organizations to monitor the network but some of them are effective against these attacks. As the cyber security is an emergent field, deals with the security of computer systems, computer networks and information transmitted over network.

To cope with these challenges and issues, efficient monitoring tool is required based on efficient protocol. SNMP was developed for the management of heterogeneous devices over the network. It is also considered as most efficient communication protocol and can also be used in monitoring due to small overheads. Our network monitoring system is also using the SNMP for efficient communication. We have used predication system for adaptive polling of information and correlation method to identity flooding attacks using anomaly detection to provide active monitoring.

1.2 Brief

In this project we have designed and developed SNMP based cyber security monitoring system. Mainly, it has two main parts: manager and agent(s) but we focused on manager. Manager also known as network management station (NMS) monitors the network devices via SNMP. It includes the adaptive polling and correlation detection mechanisms to detect the faults over the network. It monitors the network attached devices by using statistical information provided by SNMP. It also generates alerts and alarms, and also informs the network administrator about these alerts.

1.3 Scope

SNMP based cyber security monitoring system consist of two main modules: *manager* and *agent* but we have focused on the manger side of the monitoring system. Manager Is the software application running on administrator system while agent is the program running on managed devices. Manager communicates with agent(s) to retrieve statistical information using SNMP protocol. Agent stores the information in its local database also known as Management Information Base (MIB). Manager uses series of different commands (discuss later) to retrieve information from MIB and uses this information for detection of different faults and issues. Manager includes the service running for capturing the traps or alarms generated by different agents. It also includes prediction time and attack classification algorithm for polling of information from different agents. In this project I have learn about Management Information Base (MIB) along with Structure Management Information (SMI) and understand the working of SNMP protocol for the designing and development of SNMP based cyber security monitoring system.

Chapter 2 : Literature Review

In few past years, networks in the organizations increased and still keep on increasing with the addition of series of devices from different vendors. Typically, most of the networks are comprised of switches, routers, hubs, servers, hosts and printers etc. Management and monitoring of networks become an important task for organizations with the increase in size and complexity of the networks. For this, most of organizations used different tools of their choice to accomplish the task of management and monitoring. Organizations invest more on monitoring and management of their networks as the size and complexity increases. Most of the management and monitoring tools are either proprietary or open source and requires regular updates for their correct working.

Computer Security known as cyber security is the emergent field of information technology due to its reliance to different computer societies [13]. It is mostly applied to the computer, computer networks, and data transmitted or stored over them. It includes all those mechanisms and processes by using which hardware system, services or information is protected from unauthorized or intended access, modification or destruction and applies security mechanisms to guarantee the security triad given in the figure-1 below.

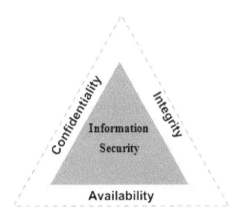

Figure 1: Information Security Triad

Network monitoring becomes more important as the networks grow in size and as well the numbers of security threats are increased to networks. Large numbers of software for network monitoring are available in the market but few of them handles the computer security issues. For this, most of the organization prefers the network monitoring tools which are using the efficient methods.

SNMP is application layer protocol and part of TCP/IP protocol. It is considered as an efficient protocol to be used in most of the network management and monitoring tools. It enables the administrator of the network to manage and monitor the networks easily by using SNMP based tools. The more details about SNMP are discussed in the further chapter.

This section describes the literature review about network management, network management systems, network monitoring, computer security and different network monitoring tools which I have used for understanding the system requirements.

2.1 Network Management

Managing and controlling the large network with diverse devices from different vendors cannot be done easily by human. The automated management tools for this purpose are required to deal with complexity of such networks. As the structure of the networks become complex, heterogeneous and large; the cost of network management also increases. Standardized tools are needed in order to control the cost of network management that can be used across the diverse devices such as routers, switches, hubs, servers, and hosts etc. from different vendors. SNMP protocol is developed to provide a tool for interoperable management of network.

2.1.1 OSI Management Functional Areas

OSI management functional area's study is helpful in developing details of a network management facility and breakdown of requirements is helpful in overall design process. International Organization for Standardization (ISO) defines the functional requirements for OSI model. The functional areas are described as;

a) **Fault Management**: Fault Management is the functional area of network management which enables the isolation, detection, and correction of abnormal operations in OSI environment.

b) **Account Management:** Account Management is the facility that maintains the users' accounts and enables charges for use of managed objects and identifies cost of objects usage.

c) **Name and Configuration Management:** It provides, identifies, collects data and sends data tofor the purpose of assisting in providing for the continuous operation of interconnection services.

d) **Performance Management:** The performance management is the facility which measures the performance of the managed objects and effectiveness of communication activities on them.

e) **Security Management:** The functional area addresses the security measures of OSI for it correct operation and protect the managed objects.

2.2 Network Management System

A network management system provides the correction, maintenance and provisioning of computer networks. It consists of collection of tools for network control and monitoring that can be integrated as follows:

1. It has the single powerful user interface but provides user-friendly set of commands to perform some or all network management tasks.

2. It requires minimal amount of separate hardware or software, mostly all equipment required for network management is incorporated into existing user setup.

A network management system is the software installed on administrator computer and has ability to accomplish the network management tasks. It has also ability to add the hardware and software in incremental way. The purpose of designing a network management system is to view the unified architecture of entire network having address and names assigned to each device and specific characteristics and link down to system. Active nodes of the network send regular status feedback information to manager.

2.3 Network Monitoring

Network monitoring is the part of a network management system. It is usually described as the use of a system that continuously monitors the computers, computers networks, servers and notifies the network administrator about failures through some graphic user interface (GUI) or some messaging system (email). It is concerned with analyzing and continuous observing of the status of different systems. (Chiu and Sudama 1992) [14] Suggests the three main designing areas as follow:

1. ***Access to monitored information***: It defines the monitoring information and how to retrieve this information from managed device to a manager.
2. ***Design of monitoring mechanisms***: It defines the best methods to obtain information from agents.
3. ***Application of monitored information***: defines usage of monitored information and how it can be used in monitoring system.

The most fundamental aspect of network monitoring is automated network management. Most of the networks monitoring systems include trivial network monitoring components but they don't address the security components. Security features for network control and monitoring are still absent, it requires attention to address security features for monitoring.

The main purpose of network monitoring is to gather statistical and behavioral information of network elements. Network monitoring information is classified into *static*, *dynamic* and *statistical*. This classification is accordance with the configuration of computer and networking elements. *Static* information is related to configuration, *dynamic* information related to network event usually by sensors and *statistical* information is extracted from dynamic information.

Agent module is a program running over the managed devices. It is responsible for collection of local management information and sending it to management stations or central management station (monitoring station). A management station includes network management software along with applications for communication with agent(s). Information is collected from active agents; either by means of request-response mechanism (passive) between management station and agents or by means of event report mechanism also called as trapping. The important categories of network management in the area of performance are response time, availability, throughput, utilization and accuracy.

2.3.1 Fault Monitoring System

Fault monitoring system is the system that is able to detect or direct the faults quickly and also identifies the cause of these faults. The main problems in fault monitoring are due to unobservable faults, partially observable faults and uncertainty in observation. Good fault monitoring system will anticipate these faults according to the tight mechanism done mostly through polling and setting thresholds. It issues reports when particular variables cross thresholds.

Fault monitoring system use commands for isolating and diagnosing such as data integrity, data saturation, connectivity, protocol integrity, connection saturation, loopback and diagnostic test etc. It requires interactive and effective user interface for operator.

2.3.2 Account Monitoring

An account monitoring is the system which keeps track of the users of the system about their usage of the network resources. It is of the general nature in the organizations, where it is often required for either internal audit in case of public services or external audit for the purpose of billings. The network monitoring system involves in gathering more details about the usage information for proper accounting.

2.3.3 Key Benefit

Mostly network monitoring is described as a critical function of the network infrastructure of the organizations that saves the money in term of infrastructure cost, performance, and employee productivity. The key benefits of the network monitoring are discussed one by one below;

i) *Reliability:*

Network monitoring provides reliability by tracking different devices and critical systems, and preemptively notifies network administrator about faults occurring over network. For example, if server goes down or some services have been stop responding then network monitoring system generates alarming condition.

ii) *Troubleshooting:*

Network monitoring also provides troubleshooting by quickly identifying the cause of the problem. It immediately diagnoses the failed systems. This limits the downtime of the failed devices by report problems and troubleshooting rather than waiting for users to report. NMS detects and reports the problem to manager for diagnoses.

iii) *Capacity:*

Monitoring system proactively identifies that how device are used and when it requires more space on disk. It also rolls out extra capacity in a controlled manner.

iv) *Stay in know*

This allows administrator to be aware of issues irrespective of their locality.

v) *Track trends*

Monitoring system detect the problems that occur occasionally or on certain peak times is hard , but network monitoring reports these trends of performance and general health of network to administrator.

vi) *Upgrades and Changes*

Network monitoring system allows the system's changes and uses these changes to track the data changes and different attacks.

vii) *Disaster recovery*

The major problems may go undetected, if there is no monitoring system. Network monitoring system uses the disaster recovery plane to minimize the down time of failure. For example, during outage of uninterrupted power supplies batteries, during backup or hard drive failure.

viii) *Proper Security*

Network monitoring system provides proper security by performing the expensive and mission critical security functions. For example, firewall protects data and allows for secure internet connectivity. Organization must frequently identify and fix problems with client firewalls before anyone at the firm notices these problems.

ix) *Money Save*

Monitoring system reduces investigation and downtime time, which indirectly saves the money in terms that administrator, works for fewer hours. So it incurs less money spent when problems occur and increase productivity of organization.

2.4 Tools

Most of the currently SNMP based monitoring tools are freely available and some are proprietary tools. Some of these tools have low cost in terms of coding time, availability, and reusing of code but most important is their adaptability to the applications. Mostly available monitoring systems are Nagios, Observium, Ganglia, Spiceworks, Zabbix, Cacti, Microsoft Network Monitor and OpenNMS etc. System Event Management and System Information Management (SEIM) based Open Standard System Information Management is widely used monitoring system.

Different tools of the MIB-browser have used to analyze the MIB oids and variables. These tools are helpful in understanding the MIB structure and hierarchy. These tools are also helpful in understanding the information retrieved from MIB. Brief descriptions of the tools are discussed below:

2.4.1 Getif

Getif is GUI based multi-functional free network tool. It was developed by Philippe Simonet. This is one of the excellent SNMP tools that allow users to collect information from SNMP devices. It's much more than an SNMP browser. It has ability to display the information of device's interfaces and OID values. It also shows routing and ARP tables, as well as preform Traceroutes, port scan, NSLookups, and IP scan functions. This work on the devices having Windows operating systems and other OS's system as well as devices manufactured by most major network companies (i.e. Cisco, 3COM, Dlink, Nokia, etc.)

2.4.2 ManageEngine MibBroswer

Manage Engine provides the free MIB browser GUI based tool for monitoring of SNMP enabled devices and server over the network. Using this, user can view the MIB and perform GET, GETNEXT and SET SNMP operations. It supports the SNMPv1, SNMPv2 and SNMPv3.

2.4.3 Net-SNMP 5.4.2.1

Net-SNMP is a software suite using the SNMP protocol such SNMPV1, SNMPv2c and SNMPv3. It includes a suite of command line application and client library using the SNMP agent. It also supports IPv4, IPv6, etc. and other transports. It has command line interface (CLI) through which user can view the MIB information by providing the different commands such SNMPGET or SNMPWALK.

Chapter 3 : Simple Network Management Protocol

In 1988, SNMP was introduced to meet the needs of a standard required for managing IP devices. It provides the simple operation set to increase ability of the administrator to manage and monitor the network attached devices.

IP Network management consists of network management station (manager) communicate with managed devices such as routers, switches, servers, hubs, printers and so on. The software program that runs on the network elements and collects the element information is called agent. Management stations are generally administrator's computer software that displays the information of devices being monitored.

The communication between manager and agents can be considered as *two way*: the manager asking the agent for the specific information is also called as polling, or *one way*: agent telling the manager that something important happened, also known as trapping. Manager has ability to set variables of agents and read variables from agent.

TCP/IP based simple network management protocol consists of three main parts including SNMP itself.

1. **Management Information Base** (MIB) is the hierarchical database of variables or OID that the agent maintains. RFC 1213 defines MIB-II.
2. **Structure of Management Information** (SMI) provides the way to define OIDs or variables and their behavior. The list of OID and variables are tracked by agent to store it.
3. **SNMP** is the protocol between manager and agent element and define in RFC 1157.

3.1 SNMP Architecture

During the task of monitoring and management, manager continuously collecting and monitoring network devices' agents. Agents also report alarms and traps to the manager using SNMP messages. Agents also send management data to managers in the form of variables. The aim of the SNMP protocol is to perform management tasks, such as modifying and applying a new configuration through remote modification of these variables. So variables can be accessible via SNMP messages. These variables are organized in hierarchical defined by SMI and MIB. An SNMP-managed network consists of three key components:

1. Agent — program running on managed devices.
2. Managed device.
3. Network management station (NMS) — software monitoring agents.

Managed devices exchange information with manager either in unidirectional way (write-only/ traps to manager) or in bidirectional way (read by manager/ request-response).

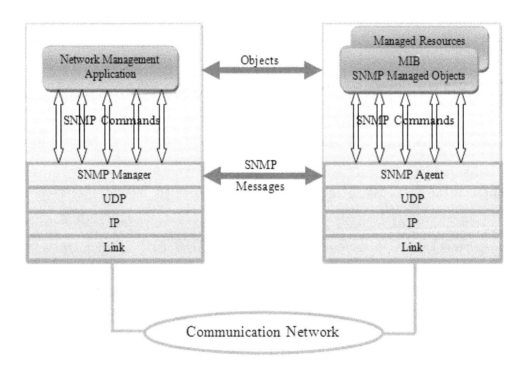

Figure 3-1 Structure of SNMP

3.2 SNMP Protocol Working

SNMP is responsible for allowing manager to perform management tasks with managed devices in the network. It has set of operations for the exchange of management information between SNMP agent(s) and manager. The detailed description of these operations and working of SNMP is shown in figure 2-2.

SNMP operates at application layer of TCP/IP protocol suite. SNMP manager send requests to the agent(s), and these requests are received by agent(s) on UDP port 161. The manager collects responses (*Traps* and *InformRequests*) from agent(s) on it UDP port 162. The agents may generate notifications from any available port. The complete working of SNMP is shown in figure2-2 below.

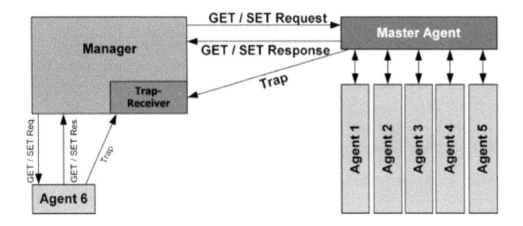

Figure 3-2: SNMP protocol working

3.3 SNMP Communication Methods

SNMP Protocol allows SNMP-capable devices to communicate their management information with each other in the form of MIB data or variables. The SNMP protocol operations used in communication are describe in next section.

SNMP enables the management of a network and allows the network administrator to easily see the status of SNMP agents running on managed devices using a network management station (NMS). There are two general techniques that are used in data communications.

3.3.1 Poll-Driven

The Poll-Driven is the general technique in which one who wants the information asks for it. In SNMP, the manager (also called NMS) would poll SNMP agents for information. In this process, NMS sends request or series of requests for information to agent(s) and agent(s) send back response to NMS in the form of MIB objects and variables.

3.3.2 Interrupt-Driven

In interrupt driven process, interrupt occurrence over the device decides to send information. In SNMP, this is referred as an SNMP agent sending information to NMS without being any query. This interrupt-driven model is used by agents to send the alarms or faults to NMS.

Both the models have their own strengths and weakness. Polling is mostly used for periodic gathering of MIB information, such as usage statistics and general status of devices. Traps are generated from interrupts that a network administrator set on managed devices. SNMP agents generate these traps when interrupt or event occurs over the managed device. Polling and traps are shown in the figure 2-3.

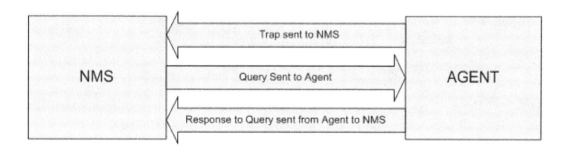

Figure 3-3: Polling and Traps.

3.4 SNMP Protocol Data Units (PDUs)

SNMP version1 specifies five core protocol data units (PDUs). Two PDUs, GetBulkRequest and InformRequest were added in SNMPv2 and the Report PDU was added in SNMPv3.

The seven SNMP protocol data units are as follows:

I. **GetRequest**: It is manager to agent request to retrieve value of a variable or OID.

II. **SetRequest**: It is manager to agent request to set or change the value of specific variable or OID.

III. **GetNextRequest**: It is manager to agent request to discover next available variables or its values. It returns a lexicographically next variable or value in the MIB using Response.

IV. **GetBulkRequest**: It is manager to agent request for multiple iterations of GetNextRequest. It returns a list of variable bindings walked from the variable binding using Response.

V. **Response:** It returns acknowledgement or response of requests from agent to manager for SetRequest, GetRequest, GetNextRequest, GetBulkRequest and InformRequest operations.

VI. **Trap:** It enables an agent to notify manager about interrupt or event by an unsolicited SNMP message.

VII. **InformRequest**: It is used for manager to manager communication.

SNMPv1 supports five PDUs, SNMPv2 supports six PDUs and latest SNMPv3 supports seven PDUs. These PDU types are further discussed in the next section along with the details about each one containing fields and format of the PDUs.

3.5 Basic Encoding Rules for SNMP Messages

Basic Encoding Rules (BER) defines the states of fundamental rules which describe the encoding of the field at byte level.

Generally, each field in BER is encoded as.

1. **Type**: Its first part and specifies data type of field by single byte identifier.
2. **Length**: It shows the length of the following data section in bytes.
3. **Data**: It consists of actual value (having number, string, OID, etc).

Figure 3-4 shows the encoding field.

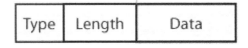

Figure 3-4: Format of basic data type encoded field

Some data types are built from the several other smaller fields like Sequences and PDUs. Therefore, a complex data types are encoded as nested fields of other data type. Figure 3-5 shows complex data type.

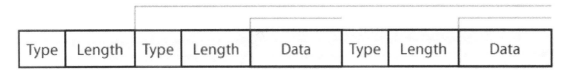

Figure 3-5: Complex Data Type encoded field

For encoding the SNMP message, two more necessary BER rules apply to encode OIDs are as follow.

1. Encoding first two numbers of OID:

The first two numbers of any OID is encoded using the formula (40*x) + y. After these two first numbers are encoded, the coming numbers in OID are encoded as a byte. Large number required special rule because one byte (eight bits) can only represent a number from 0-255. So large numbers cannot encoded as a single byte.

2. Encoding Large numbers

This scheme defines encoding for large numbers. Lower 7 bits of number are used for holding the value (0-127) and highest bit is used as a flag to inform recipient that this number consist of more than one byte. So any number greater than127 will be encoded with more than one byte. For example, 2680 is encoded as 0x94 0x78 and decoded as (0x14 *128) + 0x78 = 2680.

Primitive Data Types	Identifier	Complex Data Types	Identifier
Null	0x05	Sequence	0x30
Octet String	0x04	SetRequest PDU	0xA3
Integer	0x02	GetResponse PDU	0xA2
Object Identifier	0x06	GetRequest PDU	0xA0

Table 1: Encoding Data Types

3.6 Format of SNMP Message

SNMP message format specifies overall structure of the SNMP packet and shows the main fields included in the message. It also specifies the order of included fields. All SNMP messages are constructed as follow:

Figure 3-6: SNMP Message Format with IP header and UDP header.

Figure 2-4 show the general format of all SNMP messages. It includes the IP and UDP headers which are wrappers for SNMP messages. IP and UDP headers are not generally discussed in SNMP message format. SNMP message includes the three main fields;

1. Version.
2. Community string.
3. SNMP PDU (setRequest, getRequest,Trap,getNextRequest etc).

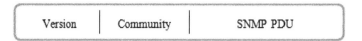

Details of the SNMP message format are shown in the table below.

Version	Integer value for version like SNMPv1 = 0
Community	It is Octet String, used to provide security to SNMP devices.
SNMP PDU	It is the body SNMP message. Several PDUs types such as GetRequest, GetResponse, GetRequest, GetNextRequest.

Table 2: SNMP message fields

Version and community in Table 2 are primitive data types but SNMP PDU is complex data type. SNMP PDU consist of several fields shown in figure 2-6. The figure 2-6 shows the PDUs of GetRequest or SetRequest and is composed of Request ID (Interger), Error Index (Integer), and a Varbind List.

3.6.1 GETREQUEST, GETNEXTREQUEST, SETREQUEST, GETRESPONSE PDU format:

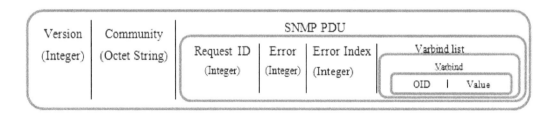

Figure 3-8: GETREQUEST, GETNEXTREQUEST, SETREQUEST, GETRESPONSE PDU SNMP message format.

The details of the SNMP message shown in Figure 2-6 are shown below in table.

Field	Description
Version	It is Integer value to identify version.
Community	Octet String used for security of SNMP devices.
SNMP PDU	An SNMP PDU contains the body of the SNMP message..
Request ID	It is an Integer value to identify particular request.
Error	It is Integer value set to 0x00 in request sent by the SNMP

	manager. Agent in response place error code in response message to manager.
	Some error codes are as follow:
	• 0x00 defines No error occurred
	• 0x01 defines Response message too large
	• 0x02 define that name of requested object was not found
	• 0x03 define requested data type A data type not matched
	• 0x04 shows manager attempted to set a read-only parameter
	• 0x05 shows general Error
Error Index	If an Error occurs it points to Object caused this otherwise it is 0x00.
Varbind List	List of variable bindings.
Varbind	Two fields 1. Object ID 2. Value for/from that Object ID.
Object Identifier	Parameter in the SNMP agent.
Value	GetResponse PDU: The returned Value from the specified OID of the SNMP agent.
	SetRequest PDU: Value is applied to the specified OID.
	GetRequest PDU: Value is a Null that acts as a placeholder for the return data

Table 3: Details of SNMP message fields.

3.6.2 Trap PDU format

Version	Community name	PDU type	Enterprise object identifier	Network address	Trap type	Specific trap type	Time stamp	Variable binding list

Figure 3-8: Trap PDU format.

The details about the fields in Trap PDU format are shown in the table below.

Field	Description
PDU type	Trap
Enterprise OID	Agent's unique identifier which is sending traps. This can be up to 255 characters in length.
Network address	Agent's default IP address that is sending the trap.
Trap type	Type of trap being sent. The following trap types with values are as follow • Authentication failure • Coldstart • Warmstart • Linkdown • Linkup • EgpNeighborLoss • Enterprise-specific
Specific	It is user-defined value or an enterprise-specific.
Time stamp	System up time shows in hundredths of a second.
Variable binding format	Discuss in next section.

Table 4: Trap PDU format

3.6.3 Variable binding format

Variable binding type: SEQUENCE_OF	Length of the variable binding	Type of object identifier	Length of object identifier	Value of object identifier	Type of value for this object identifier	Length of value for this MIB variable	Value for this MIB variable

Figure 3-9: Variable binding format.

Variable binding consists of two fields, object Identifier and value associated to that object identifier.

    a. Object Identifier: It is the OID that points to a particular parameter in the SNMP agent.

    b. Value: It is the value associated with that OID.

Figure 3-9 describes the complete format of the variable binding sequence format which is usually found in the

Varbind field in most of the PDU types.

In this chapter we have discussed the SNMP, SNMP architecture, working of SNMP protocol, SNMP communication methods, SNMP PDUs and message format of the SNMP messages.

Chapter 4 : Design and Architecture

This chapter includes the detail discussion of system architecture which we have chosen for developing and designing of the SNMP based cyber security monitoring system. System architecture defines the overall structure of the system. Designing of the system depends on the SNMP architecture. So understanding the SNMP architecture is essential in designing the architecture for our project. Design of system is defined by the series of UML diagrams, first we will define the overall architecture of the system, and then we will discuss the class diagram and sequence diagrams of the system.

4.1 SNMP based Architecture

This section describes the detail architecture of the SNMP based monitoring system. It consists of three main components as discussed in Section 2.2.

1. Managed devices.

2. Agent – software which runs on managed devices

3. Manager – application runs on the administrator system.

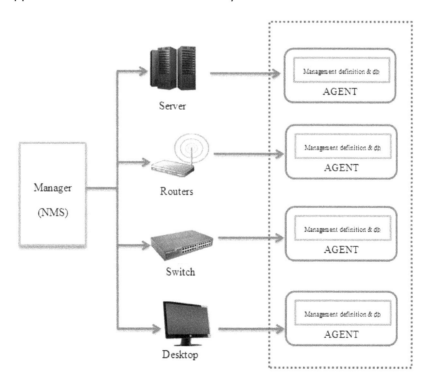

Figure 4-1: Architecture: SNMP based monitoring system

Figure 4-1 describes the detail architecture of the SNMP based monitoring system. This figure shows that different managed devices such as desktops, switches, servers and routers etc. are connected to the NMS (manager). NMS monitor all these devices using SNMP. These devices are SNMP enabled upon which agent (a program) is running. Alternative view of SNMP based monitoring system architecture is shown below.

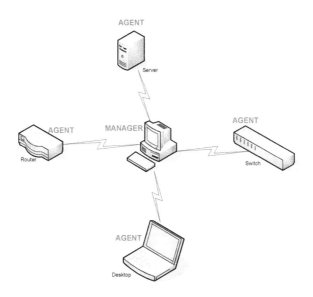

Figure 4-2: Architecture: SNMP based network monitoring system

During monitoring *manager* continuously collects information from *agents* running on the *managed devices*. Agents sense local environment of the devices upon which they are running. Each agent stores information of local environment in his respective Management Information Base (MIB). Manager uses series of commands to communicate with agents in order to retrieve and set information variables, discuss in section 2.2.2. Agents also send trap messages (PDU) when some event or interrupt occurs on device or agent. In response of manager's queries, agents send the management information to manager in the form of variables.

The aim of SNMP protocol is to perform management tasks, such as retrieving, changing or applying new setting through remote access of variables. So variables are organized in hierarchies in MIB and retrieved using SNMP. These hierarchies and other metadata are described by both SMI and MIB.

4.2 Proposed Architecture Design

Architecture design is the high level representation of the system and provides the overview of the system. Being the first stage of designing process, it represents the basic framework of the system. Our propose architecture of system identifies the major components of the system and communication between these components. The architecture diagram of system below shows the main components i.e. manager application, agent(s) and communication between them using SNMP protocol. Arrows in the diagram show the communication between components.

Figure 4-3 shows the overall architecture of our SNMP based monitoring system. It consist of one 'manager' application running over administrator computer and one or more 'agent' programs running over the managed devices. Manager communicates with agents using SNMP protocol commands and retrieves the information from agents. This communication is bi-directional between manager and agent. Agents can also inform the manager about faults by using 'Trap' command which is unidirectional from agent to manager.

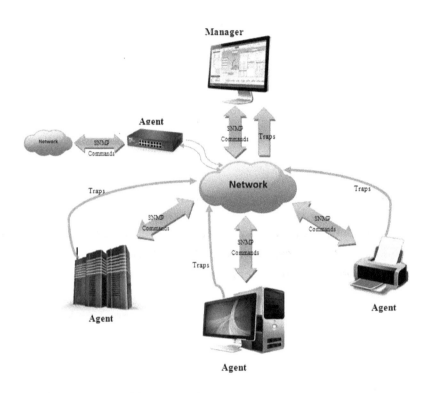

Figure 4-3 Architecture of SNMP base Monitoring System

4.3 Class Diagram

Class diagram provides the logical view of the system. It is the static structural diagram that describes the structure of the SNMP based monitoring system by showing system's classes, functions, attributes, operations and relationships among classes. The class diagram of the NMS or manger is shown below. It includes the different classes that are used in our system and their relationships with each other are shown below.

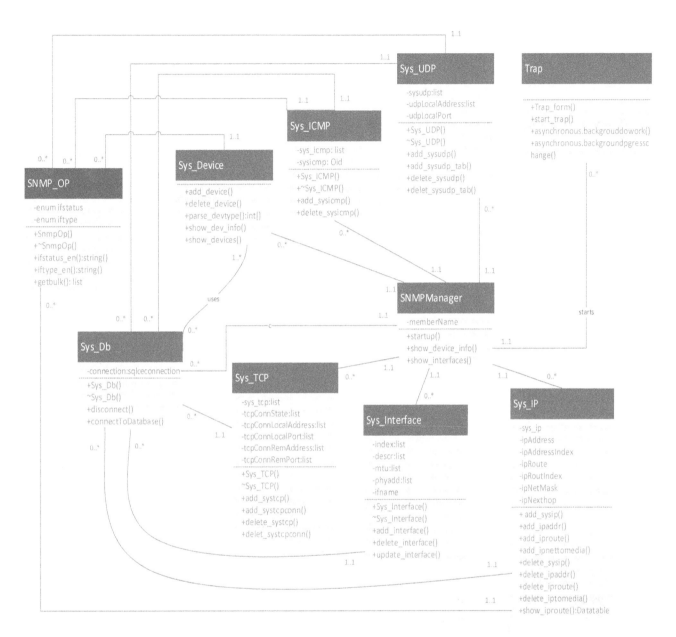

Figure 4-4: Class diagram

4.4 Sequence Diagram

Sequence diagram describes the part of logical view of the system and it is also known as a kind of interaction diagram that shows how processes operate with one another and objects interaction according to time sequence. It depicts the objects and classes involved in the scenario and the sequence of messages exchanged between the objects needed to carry out the functionality of the scenario. Sequence diagrams typically are associated with use case realizations in the Logical View of the system under development. It is also known as event diagrams, event scenarios, and timing diagrams. Each sequence diagram below shows the specific type of interaction of user with system.

4.4.1 Sequence diagram to add device

(a) Add system information

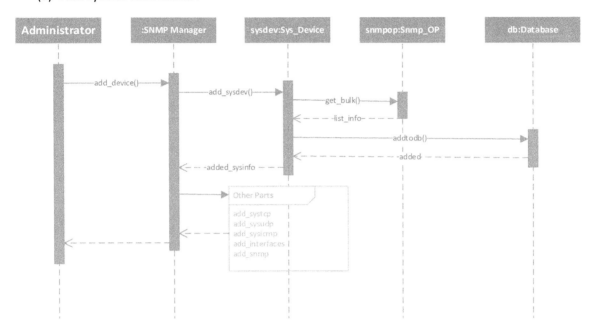

Figure 4-5: Sequence diagram to add device (System Information)

Figure 4-5 shows the sequence of interaction between different classes to add the device. This describes that administrator as external component add device by interacting with 'SNMP manager' which in turn send command to 'Sys-device' class. 'Sys-device' class retrieve information from agent (managed device), if agent is available then 'Sys-device' send information to 'Sys-db' class to store retrieved information in database. Consequently, all the information related to agent (device) such as TCP information, UDP information, ICMP information, SNMP information and SNMP information etc. is stored in the database along NMS side (manager).

(b) Add TCP information

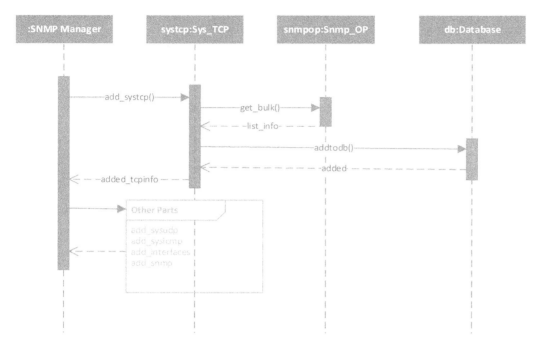

Figure 4-6 Sequence diagram to add TCP information

(c) Add UDP information

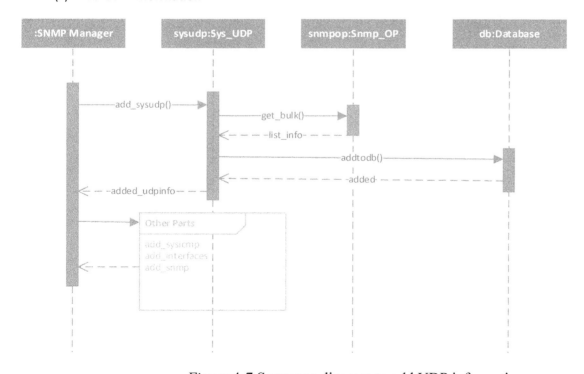

Figure 4-7 Sequence diagram to add UDP information

(d) Add ICMP information

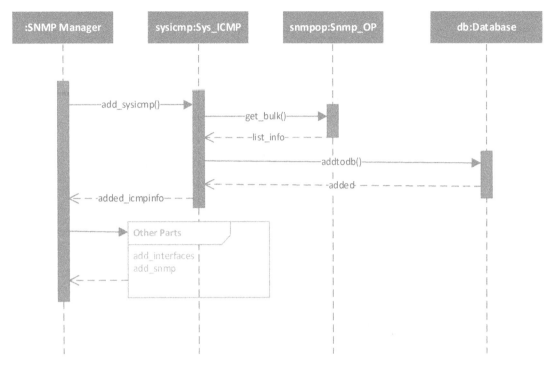

Figure 4-8 Sequence diagram to add ICMP information

(e) Add Interface information

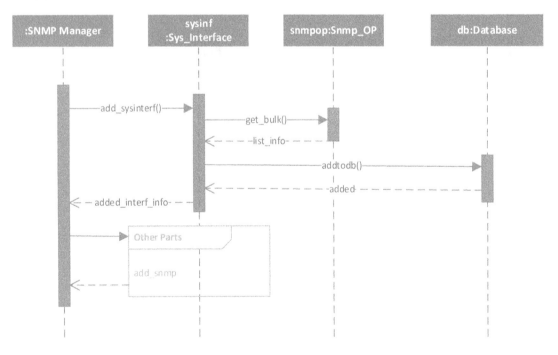

Figure 4-9 Sequence diagram to add Interface Information

(f) Add SNMP information

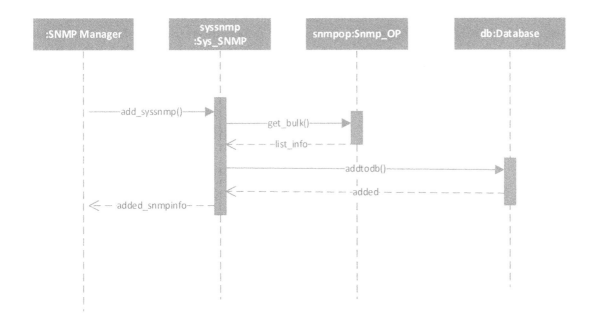

Figure 4-10 Sequence diagram to add SNMP Information

4.4.2 Sequence diagram to show information

(a) Show system details

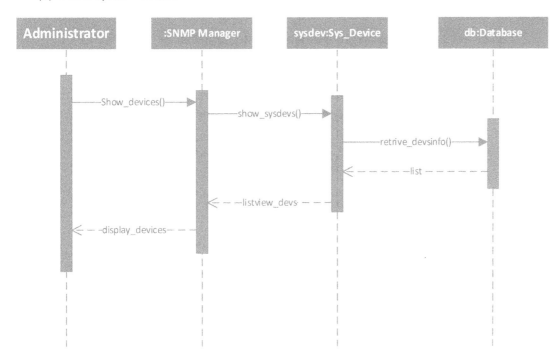

Figure 4-11 Show device information

Figure 4-11 describes the sequence diagram to show the information of added devices in monitoring system.

This diagram shows that administrator view information by interacting with 'SNMP manager'. 'SNMP manager' send command to 'Sys-device' to show information of requested device and it retrieves the information from database and send response back to 'SNMP manager'. 'SNMP manager' display this retrieved information to the administrator via GUI.

(b) Show system interfaces

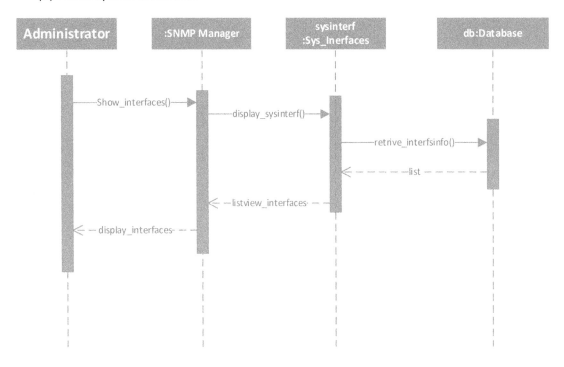

Figure 4-12 Sequence diagram to show system interfaces

Figure 4-12 describes sequence diagram to display the interfaces of the requested device. Administrator wants to see the interfaces of the specific device. 'SNMP manager send 'display_sysinterf' command to 'Sys-interfaces' class which retrieves the information of interfaces of specific device. SNMP manager display the interfaces to the administrator via GUI.

(c) Show interface details

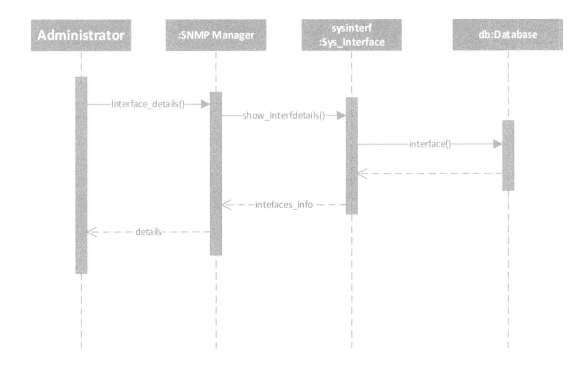

Figure 4-13 Sequence diagram to show interface details

Figure 4-13 describes sequence diagram to show details of specific interface by retrieving information from database, similarly describes in previous diagram.

4.4.3 Sequence diagram of Traps receiver

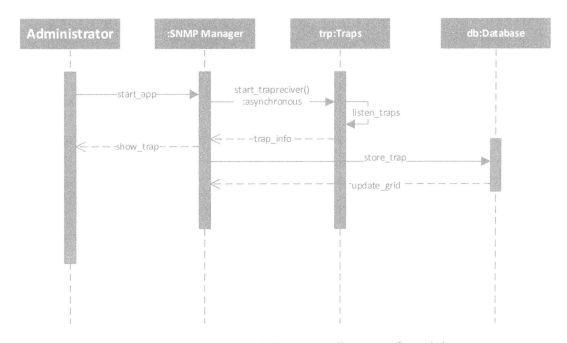

Figure 4-14 Sequence diagram of receiving traps

Figure 4-14 shows the sequence diagram of receiving traps. This describes that when the administrator start the application, SNMP manager automatically starts the service of receiving traps. Traps are uni-direction as described in section 4.1. Trap class run the asynchronous service which is continuously listening for traps from agents. When some event or interrupt occurs over the agent, agent sends traps to manager. The trap service running over agent receives traps and display to the administrator.

4.4.4 Sequence diagram of Polling

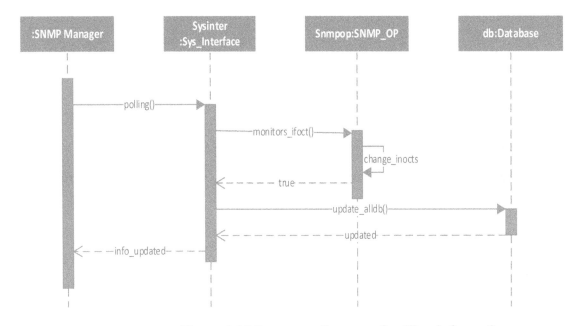

Figure 4-15 Sequence diagram of polling information

Figure 4-15 shows the sequence diagram of polling information. This describes that SNMP manager send polling command to sys-interface component which interact with snmp-operation class to poll all the information from agent. When sys-interface component receives all information then store this information to database and send message to SNMP manager that information is updated in database.

4.4.5 Sequence diagram to update information

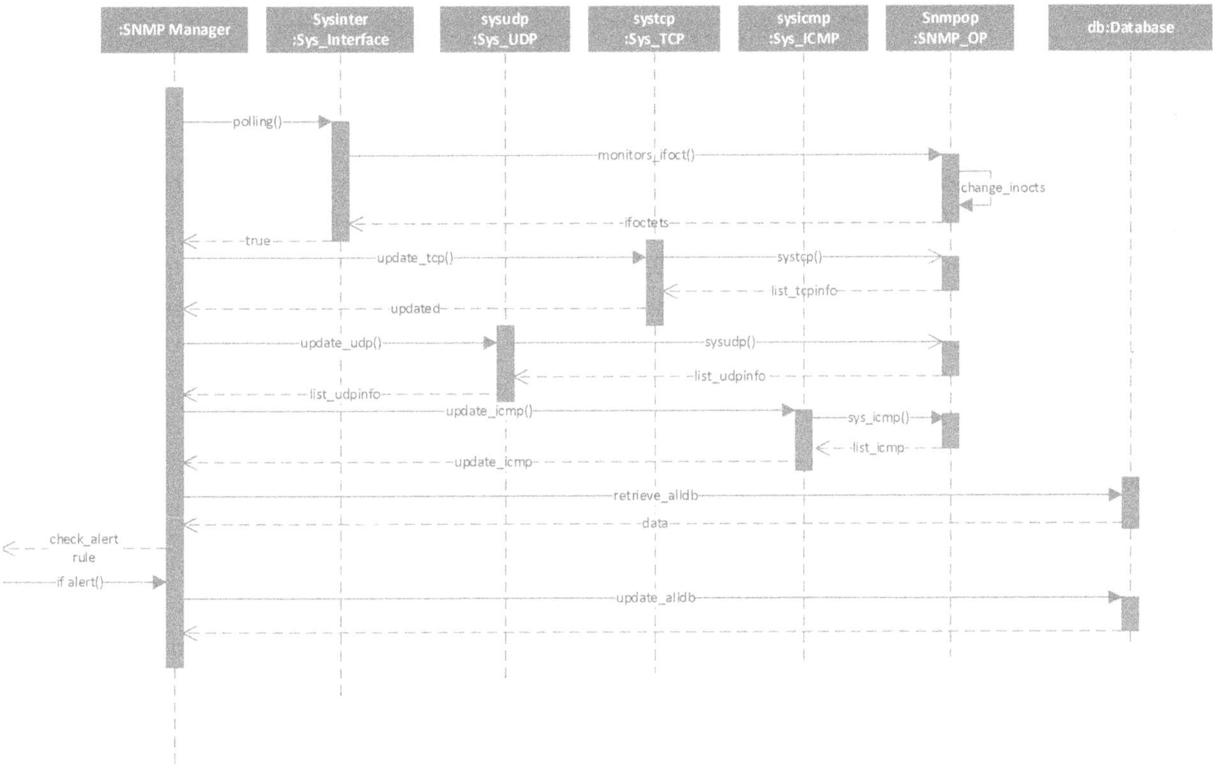

Figure 4-16: Update information sequence diagram

Figure 4-16 shows the sequence diagram of update information. This figure describes that SNMP manager is continuously polling the received-octets information from agents. When manager detects that number of received octets have changed then it polls all the information such as TCP, UDP, SNMP, TCP, and other information. The database information of respective device has updated according to new information.

Chapter 5 : Methodology & Implementation

This chapter includes detail discussion of methodology and implementation of SNMP based cyber security monitoring system. In previous chapter we have discussed the detail architecture and design of system. Methodology defines the procedures and methods chosen for research and implementation of system. In this section, we will first discuss the methodology and then system implementation supported by component diagram.

5.1 Methodology

This section describes methodology which provides an outline of research for project. It deals with associated methods and techniques used in the development of this project. The research methodology was also designed to answer some questions about the efficient methods for polling and detections or analysis of faults. The methods described here are qualitative, as they are an array of interpretative techniques, which describe and explain the overall system functions.

Aims and objectives of project are as follow:

1. To provide clear understanding of the SNMP based monitoring system.
2. Collection of valuable information to identify alarms.
3. Inform administrator about faults and alarms.
4. Use of efficient methods of polling and detection to detect cyber security related faults and attacks.

Both network monitoring and management, being critical functions require efficient methods of monitoring. SNMP protocol provides efficient methods of collection of statistical data for the management of network devices. This statistical information gathered via SNMP protocol can also be used for monitoring. SNMP based network monitoring is generally considered as an efficient protocol because of its low overheads over the network. The collected data by SNMP is worthless unless the use of efficient detection and analysis system.

The adaptive polling algorithm is used with SNMP protocol to collect the MIB data. It provides the efficient collection method by predicting the update time for MIB and collects the MIB data as it is updated on agent. This is an efficient method because it reduces number of SNMP commands over the network for polling and only sends commands when it will be required. Along with adaptive polling mechanism, attack detection mechanism is also used to detect faults. Most of the attack detection mechanisms are based on machine learning concepts to avoid DDOS attack. System produces alarms either directly by traps in case of rules violation or by attack detection system. Network device's interfaces also provide the useful information to monitor traffic and can also easily identify the fault occurrences.

This is concluded that SNMP based network monitoring is an efficient monitoring system. Along with the use of adaptive polling and attack detection mechanisms, increase its ability to monitor the cyber security faults. This system will help the administrator to identify faults and maintain the coherent network in organizations.

5.2 Implementation

This project is implemented in C# using Simple Network Management Protocol (SNMP). In order of understanding different tools have been used which are narrated in section 2.4. SNMP commands are used in project for collection of information from the different agents running on managed devices. This application is coded in C# with .NET framework 4.5 version. This application is considered as a manager running over administrator system. Application (manager) communicate with agents using SNMP commands such *get, getnext, getbulk, set*, *response*, *trap,* or *inform* etc to retrieve the MIB information.

This application shows all the added devices that are attached to the network. It shows the information of each managed device. It also shows information about interfaces, iproute, TCP, UDP, and SNMP related to each device. The detailed information of each interface can also be seen by interacting with interface. This application is also using adaptive polling algorithm for the collection of information from agents when it is needed and machine learning classification techniques to distinguish the network traffic. It also detects the faults and informs the administrator about these faults.

In implementation section we see the component diagram to get the detail view of the system's components.

5.2.1 Component Diagram

Component diagram illustrate different components of the system and there interaction with each other. The main component of the system is 'Manager' shown in the figure 5-1. 'Manager' communicates with the other components of the system. Component diagram also describe the implementation view of the system.

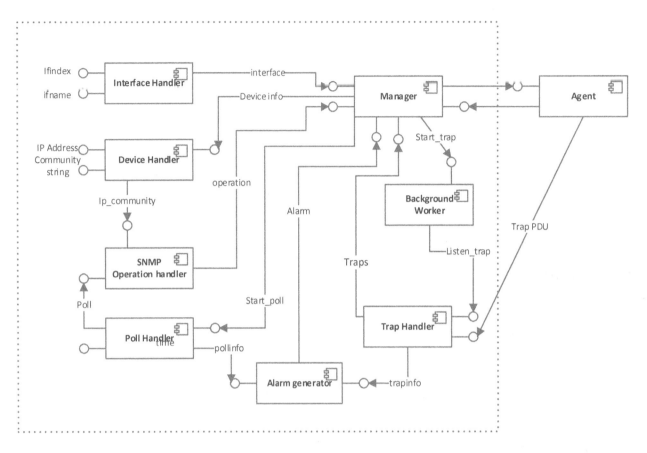

Figure 5-1 Component Diagram

Component diagram shows the communication, interaction between main components, and inputs to the components. The main component is "Manager" interact with other components. Manager starts background-worker component which sends listen-trap command to trap-handler. Trap-handler is continuously listening trap PDUs from agents and send back trap messages to Manager.

Chapter 6 : Results and Discussion

In this chapter, we shed light on results of polling and attack detection which we have discussed in the previous chapter. We will discuss polling mechanism along with it types; adaptive polling and periodic polling. We will also discuss attack detection mechanism such DDOS attack using SNMP variables. Analysis part in this chapter is supported by mathematical equation and algorithms. Results of polling attack detection are shown with the help of graphs.

6.1 Polling

Polling is the operation which refers to actively collection of information from external device by some communication mechanism. It also refers as sampling status of external devices. Polling is the process in which computer or managed devices waits for external device to check their status or information about presence. In communication, polling is the process of continuously checking other programs or devices to see their state and check whether they are still in connection or want to communicate.

In SNMP based cyber security monitoring system, polling is used to check to collect information from managed devices. Polling algorithm is running on manager and continuously checks the status of managed devices via agents. SNMP manager collects security related variables from agents using polling.

SNMP based monitoring system depends upon efficient use of polling mechanism for data collection. The efficient polling is also important for the real time monitoring of network devices. Continuous collection of information by manager from agents causes overhead due to retrieval of same information multiple times. Continuous running of polling algorithm also decrease the performance of monitoring system due to unwanted poll cycles for same information retrieval. This unwanted poll cycles can be eliminated by polling the information only instantaneously after agent's MIB has updated.

Two main problems are identified for polling of information upon agent's MIB update; earlier polling and delay polling. In earlier polling, manager polls the information from agents before it is updated on agents. This is also considered as false or unwanted polling. This causes overhead in term of bandwidth usage and resource allocation by manager for unwanted polling. In Delay polling, manager polls the information from agents after some time information is updated on agents but not immediately. Information is retrieved after some delay of MIB update on agents. Real time monitoring is also effected due to delay polling.

Polling has disadvantage to check too many managed devices and time required for polling exceeds response time or availability time of managed devices. The polling algorithm used in SNMP based monitoring is as follow,

---
Algorithm 1 : Polling Algorithm

1:    **procedure** polling_information()

2:      t ← time

3:      Number of managed devices (agents) $\hat{A}_i$ **:** i=1...n**;**

4:      **while** (true) **do**

5:          avail← **is_availabile**($\hat{A}_i$);

6:          **if** (avail = = true) **then**

7:             **poll_information** ($\hat{A}_i$);

8:          **end if**

9:    **wait** (t);

10:	**end while**
11:	**end procedure**

Algorithm 1: Polling Algorithm

Time in above algorithm can either be fixed known as periodic polling or variable known as adaptive polling. After polling information from *n* managed devices in one cycle, algorithm waits for time *t* before the start of next cycle. Algorithm checks the availability of each managed device before polling its information.

In context SNMP based monitoring system; polling can be further subdivided into two main types according to its usage, periodic polling and adaptive polling. Both types of polling along with their results are discussed in following sections.

6.1.1 Periodic polling

Periodic polling is the process to collect information from managed devices (agents) after certain interval of time regardless either agent's MIB is updated or not. Time interval for polling is specified by the administrator. Manager application waits for that interval of time and then poll information of managed devices. Periodic polling faces both problems of earlier and delay polling. It leads to the unwanted poll cycles and wastage of resources by retrieving the old information. Real time monitoring is also effected by periodic polling because information is retrieved after specific interval can be delayed.

The performance of periodic polling for different time intervals is computed out many experiments. In our project, we have added option to select one time interval for periodic polling from 5, 10, 15 or 20 seconds. The period polling of information for give time intervals is show below in graphs.

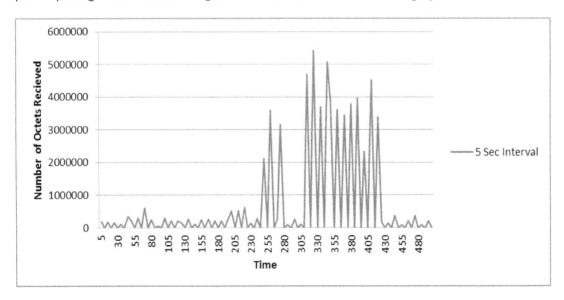

Figure 6-1: Periodic polling after 5 seconds

Figure 6-1 shows the periodic polling after 5 seconds. After each poll cycle, application waits for 5 seconds before start of next poll cycle. X-axis shows the time interval and Y-axis shows the change of octets on managed devices. Figure 6-1 shows

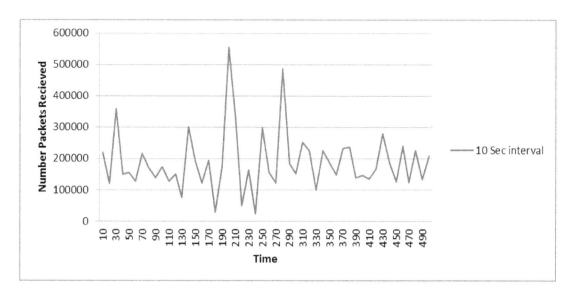

Figure 6-2: Periodic polling after 10 seconds

that application mostly polls the old information. Figure describes that number of received octet on device are mostly zero which shows that information is not updated over agent. This concludes that time interval for polling is less than update time of agents. Due to this, application experience unwanted poll cycles and wastage of resource used in polling.

Figure 6-2 shows the periodic polling of information after every 10 seconds. This shows that there are no unwanted poll cycles and manager polls the updated information from agents after each 10 seconds. The range of packets received on agents is from 100000 to 550000 packets. Average rate of packets received on agents

is 15.5 Mpps (Mega packets per second). Earlier and delay polling problems are also significantly reduced.

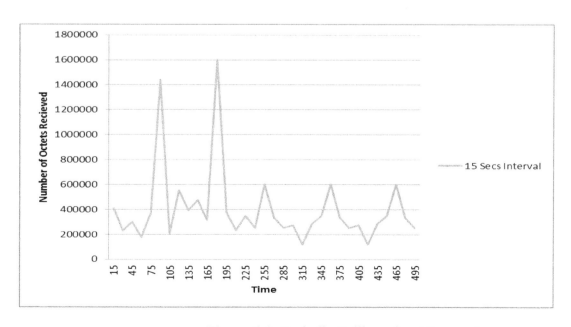

Figure 6-3: Periodic Polling after 15 seconds

Figure 6-3 shows the periodic polling of information after 15 seconds. This shows that polling is delayed because large number of packets is received on agents. The range of received packets is 170 Mpps to 1600 Mpps. Large change in number of received packets causes the delay polling problem due to which real time monitoring is also affected.

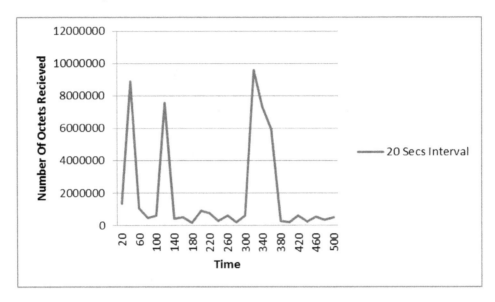

Figure 6-4: Periodic Polling after 20 seconds

Figuer 6-4 shows the periodic polling of information after 20 seconds.This describes that change in number of received octets is larged after 20 seconds and causes the delay polling.

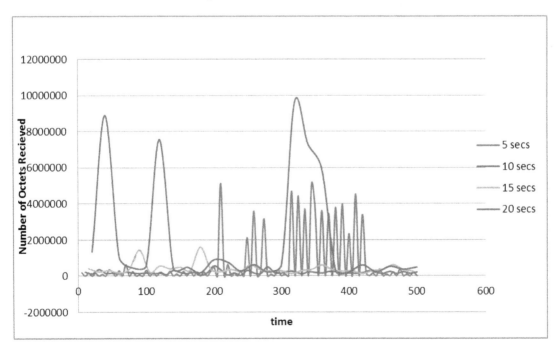

Figure 6-5: Comparison of Periodic Polling

Figure 6-5 shows the comparison of periodic polling after 5, 10, 15 and 20 seconds. This graph shows that the efficient polling is one which does not face both delay and earlier polling problems. The graph line nearer to zero but not touches zero along y-axis are considered as best polling time interval. From figure 6-5, we concluded that in periodic polling, 10 seconds time interval is best suited for SNMP based monitoring system. The reason for it efficiency is that it detect the small change in number of received octets and also it doesn't have unwanted or false polling cycles.

6.1.2 Adaptive polling

Adaptive polling is the process of collection of information from agent(s) after variable interval of time. The time interval in not fixed like in periodic polling but it is variable and depends upon the response time, bandwidth availability and update-time of MIB on agents.

In our project, manager is responsible for the calculation of time-interval in adaptive polling. Initially, we have chosen the 10 seconds as time-interval for adaptive polling because of reasons explained in previous section. After this during each cycle, manager application sends requests to agents and waits for their response. If device is not available time for wait is incremented and time at which response received is noted. Wait-time is calculated separately for each agent hosts and new time-interval for next cycle is calculated by average of wait-times of agents.

The algorithm for adaptive polling is given below:

Algorithm 2: Adaptive Polling Algorithm

1: **procedure** adaptive_polling()

2:    t :=10 seconds

3:    Number of managed devices (agents) $\hat{A}_i$: i:=1...n;

4:    time associated with each device t_i :=t ; i:=1...n;

5:    **while** (true) **do**

6:      **for** i:=1 to n devices **do**

7:          $t_i \leftarrow$ *aysnc*_**responsetime**($\hat{A}_i$, t);

8:          avail$\leftarrow$ **is_availabile**($\hat{A}_i$);

9:          **if** (avail = = true) **then**

10:                **poll_information** ($\hat{A}_i$);

11:             **end if**

12:             **wait** (t);

13:        **end for**

14:        t $\leftarrow \sum_{i=1}^{n} (t_i)$

15:    **end while**

16: **end procedure**

Algorithm 2: Adaptive Polling Algorithm

aysnc_responsetime() run as a thread for the calculation of wait-time for each device $\hat{A}_i$. It doesn't wait for the completion of thread, but as the results are received assigned to t_i. For next cycle, time-interval is calculated by taking average of wait-time for all available devices.

Algorithm 3: Aysnc response time

1:    **procedure** aysnc_responsetime($\hat{A}_i$,t)

2:    t is time for wait

3:    avail$\leftarrow$ **is_availabile**($\hat{A}_i$);

4:    **if** (avail == true) **then**

5:        $t := t - 1$;

6:    **else**

7:        $t := t + 1$;

8:        **while** (avail ≠ true) **do**

9:           $t := t + 1$;

10:       **end while**

11:   **return** t

12: **end procedure**

Algorithm 3: Aysnc response time

Algorithm 3 describes the increment and decrement in time t related to each device. If device is available, t is decremented by one and if it is not available, t will be incremented by wait-time of response received from agent. Then t specific to each device is returned to algorithm 2 from where average is taken to compute t for next cycle.

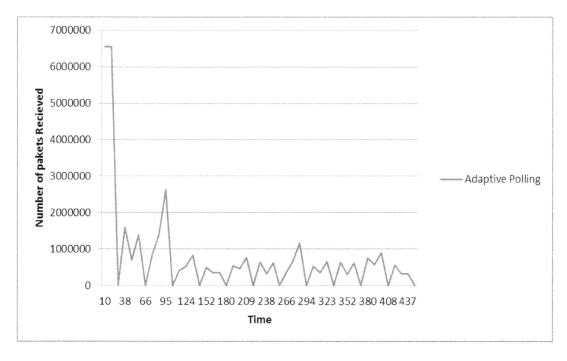

Figure 6-6: Adaptive polling

In figure 6-6, the results of adaptive polling are shown. This describes that there are some unwanted poll cycle but still it detects the minor change in number received packets over agents. Time *t* for each polling cycle is variable and depends upon the response-time, bandwidth availability, and MIB update time of agents. There are total 50 number of poll out of which 11 are unwanted or false poll. Total performance of adaptive polling is 78 % and false rate is 22%.

Adaptive Polling		
Total number of Polls	*True*	*False*
50	39	11
100%	78%	22%

Table 5: Adaptive polling

6.2 Attack Detection System

This section includes the details and discussion about the attack detection system which we have used in our project. We have used the anomaly based attack detection system using correlation of MIB data and determined detection time using adaptive polling. We have selected 16 variables from 6 groups (such as IP, interface, system, TCP, UDP, ICMP) in Mib-2 defined in RFC1213.[19] . Out of sixteen varaibles,15 MIB objects are of Counter32 data type and sysUpTime is of non-negative 4-byte integer which is continuously incremented. We have selected these 15 MIB variables which respond for the detail analysis of attack. Outgoing and incoming traffic over the agents continuously updated these MIB variables relevant to their environment.

MIB-2 Group	SNMP MIB objects
interface	ifInOctets
	ifInUcastPkts
ip	ipInReceives
	ipOutDiscards
	ipInDelivers
	ipOutRequests
tcp	tcpOutRsts
	tcpAttemptFails
udp	udpInErrors
system	sysUpTime
icmp	icmpOutMsgs
	icmpInMsgs
	icmpInDestUnreachs
	icmpInEchos
	icmpOutEchoReps
	icmpOutDestUnreachs

Table 6: MIB-II Groups and objects.

At first stage we determine the update time of the MIB to trigger the attack detection. On the second stage, we use the attack detection algorithm to detect the attack traffic. If there is possibility of attack is detected at second stage then at third stage we will further perform detail analysis of attack and determine the type of attack related to traffic such as tcp, udp, icmp etc.

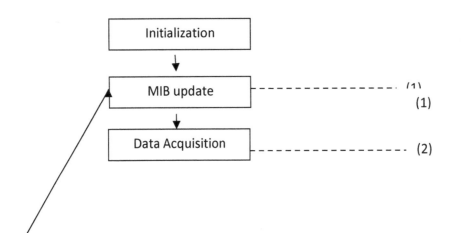

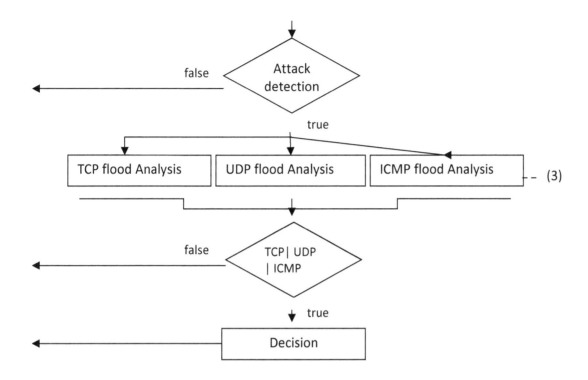

Figure 6-7: Attack detection algorithm flow chart.

Figure 6-7 shows the flow chart of detection algorithm and also describes the stages of algorithm. At first stage, algorithm depicts the MIB update-time as discussed in adaptive polling section 6.1.2. We determine the update time from adaptive polling which collects the *ifInOctets* from agents to predict the update time of MIB. At second stage, we have used symptom analysis to determine the flooding attack based on delivering ratio and amount of traffic to/from each agent which determines and distinguish normal from attack traffic.

Traffic flooding attacks on the target devices consume much bandwidth and degrade the network performance. Therefore, parameters related to bandwidth and performance on the target agents are changed when flooding attacks occurred on target device. BPS (bits per second) and PPS (packets per second) are the parameters related to bandwidth. ResponseRatio(), DeliverRatio(), and diff() functions help in the identification of attack symptoms, which based on the correlations MIB-2 objects. DeliverRatio(), ResponseRatio(), diff() and other functions are described below.

Equation and Notations	
t	one second time unit
t_n	n-th detection time
mib(t_n,oid)	MIB OID value at time t_n
diff(t_n, oid)	= mib(t_n,oid) − mib(t_{n-1},oid)

bps(t_n)	= 800 * diff(t_n, ifInOctets) / diff(t_n, sysUpTime)
pps(t_n)	= 100 * diff(t_n,ifInUcastPkts) / diff(t_n, sysUpTime)
DeliverRatio(t_n)	= diff(t_n, IpInDelivers) / diff(t_n, ipInReceives)
ResponseRatio(t_n)	= diff(t_n, ipOutRequests) / diff(t_n, ipInReceves)

Table 7: Equations and notations in attack detection

Table 7 contains some important equation and notation which we have used in attack detection algorithm.

Algorithm 4: Traffic flooding attack detection Algorithm

```
1:     procedure Boolean Symptom_analysis()
2:         initialize  weight w := 0 ;
3:         if( bps < Thd( bps )  &&  pps < Thd( pps ) ) do
4:             return false;
5:         end if
6:         if( DeliverRatio(t)  <  Thd( DeliverRatio ) ) do
7:             w := w+1;
8:         end if
9:         if( ResponseRatio(t) < Th( ResponseRatio) ) do
10:             w := w+1;
11:         end if
12:         if( Diff (t,ipOutDiscards) > Th (ipOutDiscards) ) do
13:             w:=w+1;
14:         end if
15:         if(w > =1) do
16:             return true ;
17:         end if
18:         return false;
19:     end procedure
```

Algorithm 4: Flooding attack detection Algorithm

In algorithm 4, *DeliverRatio()* function represents the ratio of packet transmitted from IP to transport layer on target device. During normal behavior of the system it doesn't exceed 80% but in case of flooding it is less 30% due to error (checksum error) or buffer overflow.

Similiarly *ResponseRatio()* in algorithm 4, represents number of response packets that the target system sends to remote hosts. During normal conditions, it is greater than 50% but in case of any attack it is below 40% which is due to the dropping of response packets. *ipOutDiscards* represents the number of dropped packets and it increases during flooding attack.

In attack detection system, several threshold values are used for distinguishing normal and attack traffic. These thresholds are related to BPS and PPS, and are computed from the number of packets generate by adversary [20]. We used these threshold for BPS and PPS variables to ensure the reliability of *ResponseRatio()* and *DeliverRatio()*. These threshold values can be static or dynamic but we have use fixed threshold values to determine the difference between attack and normal traffic for *ResposeRatio()*, *DeliverRatio()*,and *diff()*. These thresholds are shown in Table 8.

Thd(pps)	20 pps	Thd(Bps)	1 Mbps
Thd(ResponseRatio)	0 .4	Thd(ipOutDiscards)	0.0
Thd(DeliverRatio)	0.8		

Table 8: Threshold values

Rest of the MIB variables are used in attack classification as discussed in [20]. We have used this technique in our project to detect and classify flooding attacks.

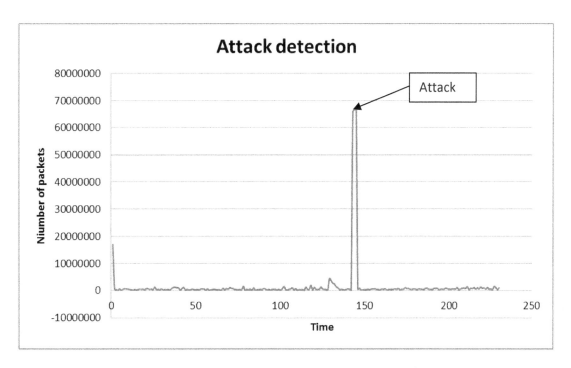

Figure 6-8: Attack detection

We have established the setup to conduct the flooding attack over the managed devices. For this purpose we have used four systems with Linux OS and different virtual machines to launch icmp, tcp, and udp flooding attack on target system. The figure 6-8 shows the icmp attack on host with 40% of packets lost rate. Our attack detection system efficiently detects the flooding attacks MIB data retrieved via SNMP protocol.

Chapter 7 : Conclusion and Future Work

7.1 Conclusion

The main objective of this project was to design and develop the SNMP based cyber security monitoring system which enables the network administrators of the system to monitor and view the different network related faults and issues. SNMP has ability to monitor and manage the network attached devices by providing the long range of statistical MIB information from agents. In this thesis, we have first done the literature survey about SNMP based monitoring systems and then we have proposed the design and architecture of the new system. Based upon proposed design and architecture, we have developed the SNMP based monitoring system having the ability to use statistical information from the MIB of agents for monitoring. We have used the SNMP capabilities to retrieve different variables from agents running over the managed devices. Periodic and Adaptive polling mechanisms are used in our project to improve the performance and reduce overheads. We have used anomaly based attack detection algorithm to detect the flooding attacks and classify them according to traffic types.

7.2 Future Work

The current implementation and design of the system act as a base for the future development of SNMP based monitoring systems in Pakistan. Our project provides the basic structure and foundation for future development of SNMP based cyber security monitoring system. Future work of our project includes the following research areas

1. Identify the cyber security variables from security devices such as firewall, IDS, IPS, snort, honey pots etc. and analyzed these variables to efficiently detect attacks over the network.

2. Improvement can be made in information collection mechanism by increasing the adaptive polling performance.

3. To implement the framework into cooperative networks [21-24].

References

[1] William Stallings, *SNMP, SNMPv2 and RMON, Practical network Management, Second Edition*.

[2] Dioglas R. Mauro & Kevin J. Schmidt, *Essential SNMP, Second Edition*, O'Reilly.

[3] W. Richard Stevens, *TCP/IP Illustrated Volume1*, The protocols.

[4] Liu, Liang, Wei Feng Wang, and Zhi Lei Wang. "*Design and Implementation of Network Devices Monitoring System Based on SNMP.*" Applied Mechanics and Materials 347 (2013): 763-767.

[5] Case, Jeffrey, et al. "RFC 1157: *Simple network management protocol (SNMP).*" (1990).

[6] Chaparadza, Ranganai. "*On designing SNMP based monitoring systems supporting ubiquitous access and real-time visualization of traffic flow in the network, using low cost tools.*" Networks, 2005. Jointly held with the 2005 IEEE 7th Malaysia International Conference on Communication, 2005 13th IEEE International Conference on. Vol. 2. IEEE, 2005 W. E. Council, "World Energy Resources," 2013.

[7] Cowie, Brad. "*Building A Better Network Monitoring System.*" (2012).

[8] Subramanyan, Rajesh, José Miguel-Alonso, and José AB Fortes. "*A scalable SNMP-based distributed monitoring system for heterogeneous network computing.*" Proceedings of the 2000 ACM/IEEE conference on Supercomputing. IEEE Computer Society, 2000.

[9] McCloghrieandM, K. Rose. *Management Information Base for Network Management ofTCP/IP-based Internets: MIB-II*. RFC 1213, 1991.

[10] Shaffi, Abubucker Samsudeen, and Mohanned Al-Obaidy. "*MANAGING NETWORK COMPONENTS USING SNMP.*" International Journal 2.3 (2013): 2305-1493.

[11] Alam, Naveed, and Muhammad Imran Sheikh. "*MONITORING OF NON-SNMP BASED NODES IN FTTC NETWORK.*" Science International 26.2 (2014).

[12] Rockwood, Ben. "*The Cuddletech Guide to SNMP Programming.*"

[13] "*Reliance spells end of road for ICT amateurs*", May 07, 2013, The Australian.

[14] William Stallings, SNMP, SNMPv2, SNMPv3 and RMON 1 and 2, Third Edition.

[15] McCloghrie, Keith. "*SNMPv2 Management Information Base for the Transmission Control Protocol using SMIv2.*" (1996).

[16] Levi, David B., Bob Stewart, and Paul Meyer. "*Simple network management protocol (SNMP) applications.*" (2002).

[17] Bruey ,Douglas. "*Simple Network Management Protocol*. RaneNote 161,2012. 15-7-2015, (http://www.rane.com/note161.html).

[18] Charles M. Kozierok. " *The TCP/IP Guide,* Version 3.0, 2005. *(*http://www.TCPIPGuide.com).

[19] IETF RFC 1213. Management Information Base for Network Management of TCP/Ip-Based Internets: MIB-II, http://www.rfc-editor.org/rfc/rfc1213.txt

[20] Park, Jun-Sang, and Myung-Sup Kim. "Design and implementation of an SNMP-based traffic flooding attack detection system." Challenges for Next Generation Network Operations and Service Management. Springer Berlin Heidelberg, 2008. 380-389.

[21] Tauseef Jamal and Paulo Mendes, Cooperative Relaying in Dynamic Wireless Networks under Interference Conditions(2014), in: IEEE Communication Magazine, Special issue on User-centric Networking and Services.

[22] T. Jamal, P. Mendes, and A. Zúquete, "Wireless Cooperative Relaying Based on Opportunistic Relay Selection," International Journal on Advances in Networks and Services, vol. 05, no. 2, pp. 116-127, Jun. 2012.

[23] Tauseef Jamal (PK); Paulo Mendes (PT); "Cooperative Relaying for Dynamic Networks", EU Patent No. EP1318236, Aug. 2013.

[24] T. Jamal and P. Mendes, "Cooperative Relaying for Dynamic WLAN," Chapter abstract submitted to WiNeMO Book (Springer LNCS Editor), Feb. 2014.

Appendix A

A1. GetIf tool

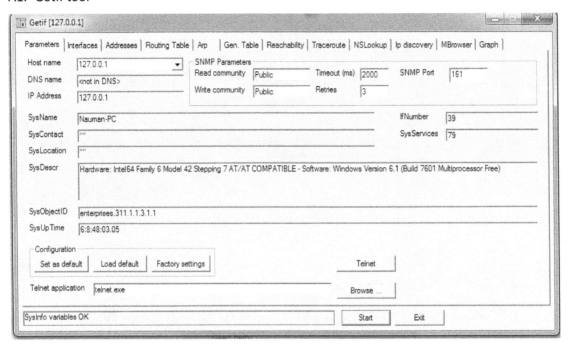

Figure 6-0-1 GetIf tool interface

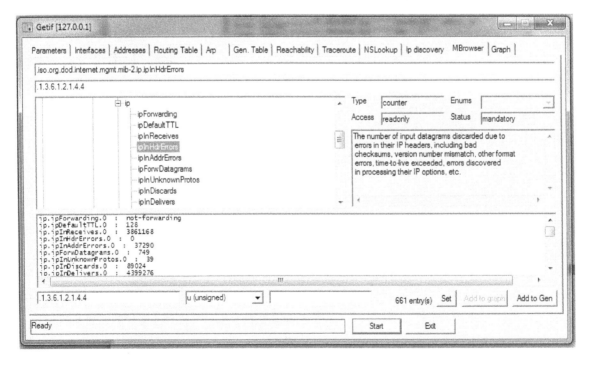

Figure 6-0-2 Show MIB with GetIf tool

A2. ManageEngine MibBroswer

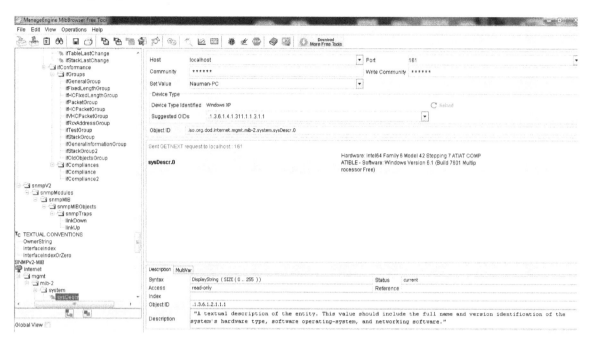

Figure 6-0-3 Mib Browser of Manage Engine

A3. Network Monitoring System (OpManager)

Manage Engine OpManager is a network monitoring software that helps large corporations or enterprise to manage their data resources and networks efficiently and cost effectively. It includes the intelligent alerting engines, configurable discovery rules, and extendable templates enable IT teams to setup a 24x7 monitoring system within hours of installation.

OpManager provides the following features

I. **Network Health Monitoring:** Monitor, visualize and resolve network or router problems. Monitor router and interfaces, bandwidth, WAN links for availability and performance. It also monitor that either router is going to critical or not. It also visualizes the CPU utilization, link bandwidth usage, memory and hard disk utilization, and power consumption etc.

II. **VoIP Monitoring:** It proactively monitors VoIP call quality across network infrastructure and ability to troubleshoot the poor VoIP performance.

III. **Network Mapping:** It automatically use L1/L2 network mapping to visualize and pinpoint the source of network outages and performance degradation.

IV. **RTT Monitoring:** It continuously monitors network link availability, latency and performance over the network.

V. **Network Configuration Management:** It has ability to automate policy-based change, configuration and compliance on your network devices across the network.

VI. **Network Traffic Analysis:** OpManger can also use flow-based network traffic analysis to monitor that how exactly link bandwidth is being utilized by users, process or application.

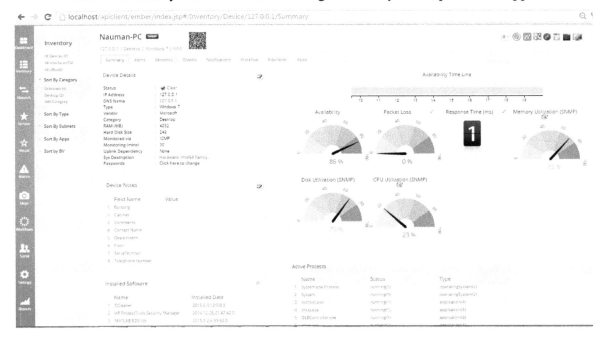

It shows the details of the device, installed software and active processes over the device. Graphs in the right side of window, shows the availability, packet loss, response time, memory utilization, and disk utilization of the selected device.

This shows the availability time and red color show system is down time period.

References

[1] William Stallings, *SNMP, SNMPv2 and RMON, Practical network Management*, Second Edition.

[2] Dioglas R. Mauro & Kevin J. Schmidt, *Essential SNMP, Second Edition*, O'Reilly.

[3] W. Richard Stevens, *TCP/IP Illustrated Volume1*, The protocols.

[4] Liu, Liang, Wei Feng Wang, and Zhi Lei Wang. "*Design and Implementation of Network Devices Monitoring System Based on SNMP.*" Applied Mechanics and Materials 347 (2013): 763-767.

[5] Case, Jeffrey, et al. "RFC 1157: *Simple network management protocol (SNMP).*" (1990).

[6] Chaparadza, Ranganai. "*On designing SNMP based monitoring systems supporting ubiquitous access and real-time visualization of traffic flow in the network, using low cost tools.*" Networks, 2005. Jointly held with the 2005 IEEE 7th Malaysia International Conference on Communication, 2005 13th IEEE International Conference on. Vol. 2. IEEE, 2005 W. E. Council, "World Energy Resources," 2013.

[7] Cowie, Brad. "*Building A Better Network Monitoring System.*" (2012).

[8] Subramanyan, Rajesh, José Miguel-Alonso, and José AB Fortes. "*A scalable SNMP-based distributed monitoring system for heterogeneous network computing.*" Proceedings of the 2000 ACM/IEEE conference on Supercomputing. IEEE Computer Society, 2000.

[9]   McCloghrieandM, K. Rose. *Management Information Base for Network Management ofTCP/IP-based Internets: MIB-II*. RFC 1213, 1991.

[10] Shaffi, Abubucker Samsudeen, and Mohanned Al-Obaidy. "*MANAGING NETWORK COMPONENTS USING SNMP.*" International Journal 2.3 (2013): 2305-1493.

[11]Alam, Naveed, and Muhammad Imran Sheikh. "*MONITORING OF NON-SNMP BASED NODES IN FTTC NETWORK.*" Science International 26.2 (2014).

[12]Rockwood, Ben. "*The Cuddletech Guide to SNMP Programming.*"

[13] "*Reliance spells end of road for ICT amateurs*", May 07, 2013, The Australian.

[14] William Stallings, SNMP, SNMPv2, SNMPv3 and RMON 1 and 2, Third Edition.

[15] McCloghrie, Keith. "*SNMPv2 Management Information Base for the Transmission Control Protocol using SMIv2.*" (1996).

[16] Levi, David B., Bob Stewart, and Paul Meyer. "*Simple network management protocol (SNMP) applications.*" (2002).

[17] Bruey ,Douglas. "*Simple Network Management Protocol.* RaneNote 161,2012. 15-7-2015, (http://www.rane.com/note161.html).

[18] Charles M. Kozierok. " *The TCP/IP Guide,* Version 3.0, 2005. *(*http://www.TCPIPGuide.com).

[19] IETF RFC 1213. Management Information Base for Network Management of TCP/Ip-Based Internets: MIB-II, http://www.rfc-editor.org/rfc/rfc1213.txt

[20] Park, Jun-Sang, and Myung-Sup Kim. "Design and implementation of an SNMP-based traffic flooding attack detection system." Challenges for Next Generation Network Operations and Service Management. Springer Berlin Heidelberg, 2008. 380-389.

[21] Tauseef Jamal and Paulo Mendes, Cooperative Relaying in Dynamic Wireless Networks under Interference Conditions(2014), in: IEEE Communication Magazine, Special issue on User-centric Networking and Services.

[22] T. Jamal, P. Mendes, and A. Zúquete, "Wireless Cooperative Relaying Based on Opportunistic Relay Selection," International Journal on Advances in Networks and Services, vol. 05, no. 2, pp. 116-127, Jun. 2012.

[23] Tauseef Jamal (PK); Paulo Mendes (PT); "Cooperative Relaying for Dynamic Networks", EU Patent No. EP1318236, Aug. 2013.

[24] T. Jamal and P. Mendes, "Cooperative Relaying for Dynamic WLAN," Chapter abstract submitted to WiNeMO Book (Springer LNCS Editor), Feb. 2014.

www.ingramcontent.com/pod-product-compliance
Lightning Source LLC
Chambersburg PA
CBHW060206060326
40690CB00018B/4277